Eugene Vesey was born and brought up in Manchester, UK. He was educated at a Roman Catholic grammar school in Manchester, Roman Catholic seminaries in the English Lake District and Midlands, the University of Manchester, where he read English Language and Literature, and the University of Liverpool, where he did his teacher training. He lives and works in London, where he teaches English as a Foreign Language. This is his second book of poetry, the first being *Venice and Other Poems*. He has also published three novels, *Ghosters*, *Opposite Worlds* and *Italian Girls*. All his books are available from Amazon. Eugene may be contacted through his Facebook page or at veseyeugene@hotmail.com.

Also by Eugene Vesey

Ghosters (novel)
Opposite Worlds (novel)
Italian Girls (novel)
Venice and Other Poems

THIRTY-NINE POEMS

Eugene Vesey

Published by New Generation Publishing in 2016

First Edition

www.newgeneration-publishing.com

New Generation Publishing

for

Marisa

Afraid

You are afraid of your
Inability to speak,
But you are only afraid of words –
Don't be afraid of words!
Trust to the spaces,
To the darknesses,
Without understanding
And be content to be;
Receive, accept, take, give,
Do not seek to feel –
Feelings are unimportant:
Be be be!
Being is birth
Not being is death;
Be and all life will come to you
And carry you away.

Armchairs

Every armchair contains a ghost,
Clothes are drapes on a lost world;
The air is full of memories not mine
And I feel like a stranger in this room,
Returning home from a future
That was without substance,
To a past that never was or will be,
Just a never-ending, everlasting present.

Beatific Vision

All their philosophies
Circulate back to nullity;
Words trigger emotions
Divergent from their meanings;
That's the moment for laughter!
Books pretend to say something
About something or other;
People put out their arms
To stop the world whirling,
The waltz of weltschmerz,
But it's just one giant cock-up!
No one can answer the riddle,
The billion-dollar question
And anyway said the spider to the fly,
Yours is not to reason why –
Yours is but to doodle, die,
And leave the Rest to Me.

Birds on Gola

Here nature is fancy-free
To fling freewheeling into its skies
Birds whose wings make music
In the heather-scented draughts
Of clear uncluttered air
Their wings and hearts beating
To the rhythm of their own
Wild and private destinies –
They won't be targets
For the games of senseless humans
Distributing death and destruction
From the barrels of their guns!

Gola is a tiny uninhabited island off the coast of Donegal, north-west Ireland, where I spent several weeks in the long hot summer of 1976. (Though it wasn't so hot in Donegal!)

Bombs

The earth is grilled
with sunlight and shadow,
The leaves are copper-brown
and gently floating down;
The river is idling
through the meadow,
The bees are buzzing
in the pollen,
And squirrels scamper
up the sycamores -
But bombs upon the town
are raining down.

By the Seaside

Gleam of sunlight
Off the gull's back;
Purple hills like bruises
On the back of the green land;
Windwallowing birds,
Fishflecked and flocked water,
Winds scampering over marram grass
And bullion rocks slime-embroidered
Little islands
Heather havens for worldfowl
Mystic shadows on the lens
Eartheaten wood
Gravel paths through ditched bogs
Trenched with earth's black blood
Gaunt gullies, chasms, coves
Mica-glinting pebbles
Stony pools crab-infested
Water bashing in blue bursts
Grunting grovelling gruelling
Groaning galloping gadarene
Gasping thrash of ocean
Pent-up aeons of force
Against pillars of cliffs
Glum and sullen sea
Not scrotumtightening
Playful, frolicking sea,
Lolling, bowling,
Swirling, swaying,
Growling, dog-vicious
Clawing the sky
Ripping land to ribbons.

Christ Is Dead

Christ dead on the altar slab
The priest huddled wizard-like
Over the alabaster corpse
Murmuring Latin incantations
Divine sorcery
Christ stretched dead at the pale feet
Of the distraught god-mother
With the moon and stars at her head
Eternal rivers of tears from her eyes
Her voice a shriek in the wilderness
Eli lamma sabacthani
A black hole in spacetime
Until with a touch of sacerdotal fingers
Godwand strikes
A current of lightning grace
Galvanizing the body
Eyelids open
Limbs stir
Battery of divine grace
Mysterious coil of eternal life
Unleashed in the heart
Splitting the rock
Fission of time atom
Fall-out of infinity
Earth a grain of grit in space
Phosphorescent with divine grace
Spinning through the universe
Shining luminously
Consecrated particle
Figment of divine imagination.

Colours

Colours of happiness in
The prism of the brain;
Conflicting and conspiring
Fragments of life
Assume sporadic harmony.

Hand on the heart
Hoping for growth to blossom
Beyond the barren wood
And for music
Not the clang of the iron hammer
Upon the stake
Not again the topple and terror
Of swinging dark
Or the barbed blood
And faces falling into ash.

Oh for a few roses in the garden
A smile from the stars in heaven
A dawn deepening down the day.

Darkness

Darkness dripping like ink
Upon the disc of memory
The needle falls softly
Everything is silent now
Except for the wind
Whimpering through the trees
And the ever-sibilant sea
Playing back memories
Of other times and tides
Memories of dreams
That never even happened
Memories of other worlds
Where I could never be
So now I'm lost and alone
Just a castaway upon
Lonely Planet Me.

Day after Day

Day after day follows day after day
After day after day after day …
Each one a tree in the forest;
One by one each tree falls
To the giant lumberjack's axe
Till no trees are left
And there's no hiding place for you;
So down you lie like a hunted animal
On the black hungry earth
And wait for the axe's final fall,
Hoping it will be swift not slow.

Each Night Without You

Each night without you
Is like a long dark tunnel
To tomorrow without you.

Tomorrow without you
Is like a big black hole
In space without you.

Heaven without you
Would be like hell
On earth without you.

Life without you darling
Is like a long, slow death
Of dreams without you.

And dreams without you
Are like nightmares
In the long lonely night.

Finger Nails

Finger nails drumming
The world's orbiting skull;
Skulking in the crypt
Of Golgothan dark
Sick and reptilian eyes;
The sunsprung icicles
Shafts of lancetlight
Through the blighted
Heart of the universe;
Quiver of starshock
Through the shorting brain,
Through the eye of the needle
To Hell.

Radius of time is gone,
Radar searching for truth,
Track of divine grace
Around the coil of space
Has rent the world's sides;
Words that once split the skies
Like thunder and lightning
Drift like snowflakes in space;
Music from the museum
Eternal ghost spreads its dark wings
Inverted paraclete
Over my world.

I Close My Eyes

I close my eyes and see
The raven perched
Upon my stomach,
At the centre of his circular eye
My fate;
Here a dozen ravens rise
With charred-paper wings,
Out of the forest
Of the night;
The moon waits with bleary eye
Upon the horizon of my soul;
A tear of colourless blood drips
From its opaque iris
Upon the forest fringe –
My spine's a river of ice.

Jungle

The matted jungle is shrunk
Weed in the drift
Grain in the warp
Gravel in the womb
Stargrit in the eye
Aeons of horror to be or not
To be have blown in one
Bursting of a sacred vessel
The silence like a worm
Has settled in the bone
The tick the everlasting moment
Bomb of time within the brain
And still the rage
Of the clanging tooth
That tolls the tax of time
Still the stalking mist
Around the borders of my brain
My palpitating heart
Deadsea fruit
Taste of life's dejected rind.

Life

Life is short
And dearly bought;
Don't throw away
A single day!

Love is rare,
A necklace fair;
Let's not unfurl
A single pearl!

Dreams are dust
But dream we must,
Or death we'll die
Before we lie!

It's a game,
No one's to blame;
We cannot win,
It's such a sin!

Loneliness

Loneliness held him by the heart
A hundredweight of sorrow;
Love seemed a pale dim vision
In the silent surrounding dark;
A sudden motion of her arm
Moved the darkness momentarily;
Two soft eyes and a simple smile
Sent a beam of love toward his heart –
But then she turned away again
And disappeared back to dark.

Lost

Door into the dark
A knife of moonlight
Slicing the glum forest
Interior of my heart.

Bats flitting through
The voiceless sky
Clouds throw shadows across
My mind's eye.

Stepping into the silhouettes
Of memories
Past the effigies
Of imagination.

I tread down the distant
Rows of stones in the graveyard
Stones with no names
My name on all of them.

Minds

Minds are not bound
By earth or flesh, sea or sky,
The electric invisible field
Of imagination
Which gardens dreams
And their corollaries
Desires.

Each man swims in the bowl
Contemplating with glazed eyes
The film of the real world
Passing between him and his ideals;
He is transfixed and mesmerised
By the eternal impossibility
Which for him lasts only a lifetime
An atom in the infinite loop of time;
His shortlived senses record
For a few seasons
And are unplugged,
All memories erased
Including memories of him.

Miry

Like a shooting star
Across the night,
Our love flashed and flew;
But now the sky
Is dark again,
My life a void,
Devoid of you.

My Angelina

My girl Angelina
Has planted a seed in my heart
That has flowered into a lovely rose,
But a rose without thorns!
Or should it be
A lily of the valley?
For she is pale and lovely
And we are in a vale of tears;
Her name is Angelina
And there is an angel inside
My Angelina, a little angel,
Who has flown on wings of love
Like an arrow to my heart
And stolen it away
To make me her hostage
With no ransom to pay!
But flowers and angels
Are only fancy thoughts,
While Angelina is so real
As real and bright as diamond,
Her light as laserlike as a distant star
Shooting from the darkness
Across life's lonely spaces
Into the dark and empty
Chambers of my heart,
Re-igniting all the dreams
That used to glitter there
And lighting up the night
That had settled on my soul.

My Precious Pearl

My head and heart are in a whirl,
My soul is in a spin,
And all because I've met a girl
To put my future in!

She has no face that I have seen
No earthly form, but wait –
Yet still I want to make her queen
Of all my world and fate!

I knew it when I heard her speak
Down in my deepest soul,
She was the one I'm meant to seek
To make the jigsaw whole!

I only wish we'd met before
Instead of now; but then –
We may enjoy it all the more,
Not knowing why or when!

I only know and only care
I've found my special girl,
The dream to dream I used to dare
Is now my precious pearl!

Nets

Nets trawl the seas of life
For dreams that slip
Like mercurial fish
Through the spaces
Of our lives and then one day
We wake with shock to see
Our lives are full of holes
Just like Blackburn Lancashire

Plea

My words may be like certain stars –
When they reach you they may be dead;
Listen instead to what I do not speak,
The pulses of my hopeless heart.

Radio

On the radio the violins giggle and croon
Beneath the light of a silvery moon;
The light of stars is about the room,
As I listen to the traffic's snorting vroom;
And the tick-tock of egotistic time
Upon my travelling-clock.

Sladjana

Sladjana
In spite of yourself
I love you still
The past gathers like ice
Around my heart
To preserve you there
Your flesh shines
In my memory
I never touched you
The way I would touch you now
You pressed me
And produced the vintage
Of my life
Sladjana
We were both young
Crazy and blind
Music plays on my mind
I loved you though
You laughed at those words
They resound through
The empty halls of history
Which I haunt like a ghost
In search of you
Let us go down together
Into the ocean of night
That we call life
And breathe each other's breath again
My life is dead without you
And I cannot rub you out
Do you know what you have done to me

There is only one globe
I see only one tree one hand
One moon on the shore
Grey light bright as lead
Your silhouette is all I see
But my darling
I would rather be
There with you
Than here
With me

Smiles

Your smiles melted the ice
Around my heart with their warmth,
Your fingers opened me like scalpels
Resected the cancer of my cares;
Your words fell like summer rain
On the Sahara of my soul;
Your smiles swept me away
Like a river in full flow ,
Over the waterfall of love
Into the whirlpool below.

Snake

There is a snake
Coiled within your rotten heart;
It was deep in the dead of time
When you were born,
Maggots fester
In your bulging brain;
Your blood was distilled
From black clouds
On a midnight
Deep in the dead of time
Before life swilled over
The sun’s blackstained face
And plunged the world
Into golden poisonous light;
You were to have been born
Within yourself eternally –
It was your plan;
And now like flakes of ash
Your dreams descend
Fluttering in the sun’s sickly face,
You shudder and twitch a stranger
In this world of son et lumière:
Your soul is like a nuclear bomb
In your world-hammered skull
Your fingers float through far-flung galaxies
Your eyes are dead stars
But the earth holds you on its barbs
Grabs you in its shark’s teeth;
You are the child of night and sea
You revolve in the centre of your mystery
But do not worry –

Speed ever faster around
Your centre of wordlessness
Each eternal moment
Will settle you there
And you will be your own self
Inside a seed of meaning
That no rockets could reach:
That is your heaven and your haven
Where you spin in dizzy joy.

So Fleet of Foot

So fleet of foot is our fate,
Like arrows the years pass;
If we don't want to be too late,
We should live each as if
It were the last.

So Let Me Cease

So let me cease upon the midnight –
Death would be a consummation
My mind would drown in darkness
The sea would sweep me away
And in that moment
Our marriage would be complete;
You would be no more outside me
I would be no more outside you
Our tongues would touch at last
Without the babble of words;
Our eyes see only the dark
Our ears be full of sounding sea
The tide of timeless night
In which we spin but once –
So let me cease to be.

Spring's Sweet Breath

Spring's sweet breath
Has whispered sweetly
Green leaves onto stiff stalks
Flowers upon the frozen fields
Of the crusty earth.

I have walked across the rims
Of seasonless worlds
Ringed with the shadows of
Perpetual unknowability.

Yet there is a solace in sunlight
A shimmer of hope in the rainbow
That dispels the bile from the bowels
And the grey gases from the brain.

sunset by the lake

in the pot of night
stars simmering
muddering waves
wind's breath
warm and cool
skein of sky
sultry mists
moonslips seawards
dusk deathening
drills of moondribbled waves
slabs of slouched hills
laving the shore
bye bye daystar
limping lamp
glass dancing jellymoon
slurping and trilling
troublesome sea

ravening night
cloth of dumb darktide
secret shore of heaven
bay of dreams
beneath ball of day
stripped switched scalding
scum of the earth
sea's sump
rocking to and fro
bowels of bestial beauty
belly of thc god
song of slinking night
waxen moon
dripping and ladling

diluted light
cupped in earth's embrace
swilled in the soup
thickening silence
laying its crop
sprouting out of fissures
anal space
soaking up beliefs and visions
into the clouds of unknowing
laying its crops of stars
on the world
streaming dreams
from men laid under rock
under the eternal pole
diving out of the sky
stricken through the heart
by the light of truth
waves lisp and slither
over the lip
land dips dizzily
down the dangerous depths
ships sliding into one
day becomes night
world turns on its spine
spins through the spell
of universal laws
down and up the hours
roll upon roll
forwards and backwards
around the riddle
tossing and tumbling
shadow slits
cut from nightlight
candles in the eyes
slanting out of hell
slicing the heart

soft and sly and seeping
over the senses
shallow brim
earth sups
juice of darkness
into every pore
night becomes a negative
in the stiff hand of space

Telegraph Lines

The telegraph lines are down
But new hills have rolled,
New rocks rung, new green grown,
And always time is still,
The sonic sea of sensations
Tiding wayward thoughts to
The scything shore of the brain;
The past ground into grey grains
And flakes have fallen fruitlessly
And furtively on the moon,
For within are seeds of other stars
And the revolutions, rolls and reels
Of the vessel whose fuel is change,
Whose only lode is the ever-flowing future
To destinations undesigned but dimly dreamt
In the mirrors of the telescopic mind.

Sorrows are wrapped in joy,
The end in the beginning,
The straightest line is a segment
Of the cylindrical circle;
Time may be finite, fickle-bladed,
But some moments fly like atoms
Into the electric charge of imagination,
Which is the battery of the soul.

The Ranges of the World

He rides the ranges of the world,
Lassoing stragglers from the word;
He rounds them up upon the plain
And herds them on salvation's train.

Life

Tell me not in mournful numbers,
'Life is but an empty dream!'
For the soul is dead that slumbers,
And things are not what they seem.

Henry Wadsworth Longfellow

Oh, dear, this little life of ours
To me indeed does sometimes seem,
A light that flickers a few short hours,
Exactly that ~ an empty dream!

Eugene Vesey

Thought For The Day

Ain't nothin' you can do,
Ain't nothin' you can say,
To change the fact that night
Is followed by the day.

Ain't nothin' you can do,
Ain't no way you can fight,
Against the fact that day
Is followed by the night.

Ain't nothin' you can say,
Ain't nothin' you can do,
To stop the grim reaper
Coming just for you.

Navigation

Through life's fearful navigation,
  Love is the only consolation;
So let love be your guiding star
  As you travel the world near and far;
Waves will come and waves will go,
  But love will beat them, high or low;
Love is brighter than lightning's flash,
  And love is louder than thunder's crash;
Love is deeper than the deepest sea,
  Makes love's path as smooth can be;
No wind can blow love's sails off track
  No rock can wreck or break its back;
So let love be your guiding star
  As you travel the world wide and far.

Time

Time is telling me
That you have gone
Rocketing away
A million miles a second
I hear your voice
In the wind
See your face
In the water
Do you ever look back?
Time sits ticking in our hearts
An unexploded bomb
If I reach out
I touch only stars
If I reach in
I find only
The space where
You used to be
And debris of dreams
I thought time was a healer
But it only tells me over and over again
With its tyrannical ticking of the clock
You've gone you've gone you've gone ...

Tottenham Cemetery

Cherry trees
And cemeteries
Death at home
In Tottenham
Two babies in a car
Don’t know who
Or where they are
A man’s feet
Upon the street
Circle back
To find the track
Thoughts that move
In the same old groove –
Life’s just a riddle
Me in the middle

Voices

Their voices echo strangely
Around the midnight strand
Their shadows stalk the moonlight
Their groping hands claw the clouds
But only ashes fall softly on their head

When the lights go out
Silence reigns and rains
And with the dawn
Come new rains
To wash the world anew –
Pitter patter
Prattle of rebirth
Excited whispers
Around the earth
That was clogged with black blood
Caked with salt of tears
Tears of terror gone

The earth gasps with relief
Rescued from destruction
It sprouts new blooms
And goes its merry way

For information about Eugene's other books, please see over.

GHOSTERS

GHOSTERS is the prequel to both *Opposite Worlds* and *Italian Girls*. At the age of twelve, Frank Walsh leaves home in Manchester and enters a Roman Catholic seminary in the English Lake District to fulfil his dream of becoming a missionary priest. At twenty-one, having lost his faith, he makes an unsuccessful attempt to commit suicide, leaves the seminary and returns home. With the help of Sally, the girl next door, he slowly manages to recover from depression and starts to feel 'normal' again. After finishing university, he leaves home yet again – and Sally – to live in London. There he tries to escape the ghosts of the past and fulfil his dream of being a writer, while teaching English to foreign students in a private school in Soho. He has a passionate love affair with one of his students, Marina, a vibrant, eighteen-year-old Yugoslav girl. They plan to marry, but a chance meeting with a ghost from the past threatens to destroy this dream too. Yet Frank refuses to be beaten, because he still has one dream left …

'I like it ... imaginatively strong ... I was riveted ... sensitively worked out ... intelligently written ... powerfully presented ... this heart-felt painful re-creation of a central hidden part of our culture.'
Kate Cruise O'Brien, Poolbeg Press Ltd., Dublin

'... extremely well-written and moves at a pace that keeps you captivated. Crucially, it deals with the disturbing subject of abuse in the Catholic Church in a revealing but sensitive way, without pulling any punches, drawing on the author's own first-hand experiences ... provides a graphic and disturbing insight into the emotional traumas suffered by both the victims and ironically the perpetrators ... an informative and thought-provoking book that could and should be adapted into a television drama.'
John Vesey, Amazon

'This novel deals with some very sensitive and difficult (not to say topical) issues in a very interesting, serious, intelligent way. It's very well written. It's obviously autobiographical, but that in no way invalidates it. The story really carried me along and I couldn't wait to find out whether Frank would be able to turn his life around or not. I won't give the game away by saying whether he does or not! The writing style is unshowy, verging perhaps on plain, but that for me gives the story an extra patina of truth. The story is so engaging that it doesn't need any embellishments of any kind in my view. I'd recommend this book to anyone who is interested in a very good human story, well told, and who is interested in such issues as child abuse, religious indoctrination, love and self-fulfilment. It is a bit slow at the start, but I found it difficult to put down once I got into it.'
Orinoco, Amazon

'Christian romance is a bit misleading perhaps, but this book does deal with the question of religious faith – specifically the Catholic faith and theology – in a very intelligent, dramatic and moving way. More accurately, it deals with the loss of faith. The main drama is about how Franks Walsh manages to recover from his drastic loss of faith, reinvent himself and forge a new life, in effect a new identity. But the story also encompasses other themes, such as child abuse [very topical] and romantic love both homosexual and heterosexual. I found the story of Frank's progression from despair at losing his faith (and therefore his vocation to the priesthood) to relative happiness as a young, carefree teacher in London to be completely engrossing. The author deals with all these themes very honestly – sometimes painfully honestly – so for me this was a riveting read.'
Nena, Amazon

'Wow! Brilliant! Especially if you're Polish and Catholic like me. Well, I should say 'lapsed Catholic'. This story reminded me why I no longer believe. Every Catholic bishop and priest should read it. So should every parent who tries to indoctrinate their children with any strange, supernatural

beliefs – in the end it's likely to be counter-productive. I could identify so closely with Frank even though I'm not a man. My own story is almost parallel. When I was reading this book I felt as if I was looking in a mirror! I actually understand myself better now. That's what good literature should do, isn't it?'
Polish Student

'Ghosters has a really powerful emotive effect, as it charts Frank Walsh's life throughout his childhood and as a young adult and is very truthful and honest. It deals with faith, religion, love and most of all, identity. It is an empowering story that allows the reader to connect to Frank, the main character. This was a thoroughly enjoyable read that grips the reader throughout.'
Miss A. M. Kearney, Amazon

Amazon Average Customer Review *****

OPPOSITE WORLDS

OPPOSITE WORLDS is the follow-up to *Ghosters*. It finds Frank Walsh alone and lonely in London, having been jilted by his Yugoslav girlfriend, Marina, on their wedding day. On the rebound from this, he has a passionate affair with Kalli, a gorgeous Greek singer and belly-dancer, who is a student in his class at the school in Soho where he teaches English to foreign students. When Kalli leaves him, Frank finds himself alone again. Then one evening, in a folk club in an Irish pub, he hears a young, attractive girl singing and falls instantly in love with her. Her name is Mary, he contrives to meet her and Mary falls in love with him. Love leads to marriage – reluctantly at first on Frank's part – but their marriage proves to be a collision of two very different, indeed opposite, worlds …

'... an extremely well-written book – thoughtful, descriptive and emotive. The journey of exploration and discovery of Frank Walsh enables the reader to identify with him on a deep emotional level. As you read, you feel how Frank is thinking and feeling as if you're in that moment with him. Overall, it's a great read as it explores identity, relationships and belonging. A definite recommendation! It gives a clear insight into the life of Frank Walsh and touches the reader on a deeper level.'
Miss A. M. Kearney, Amazon

ITALIAN GIRLS

ITALIAN GIRLS is the third instalment of Eugene Vesey's trilogy about Frank Walsh. At the end of *Opposite Worlds,* the prequel to *Italian Girls,* Mary, Frank's wife, has left him, frustrated by his philandering ways and apparent infertility. Unlike Mary, Frank doesn't believe in marriage, nor does he believe in God any more, though like her he was brought up as a Catholic. He even spent nine years training to be a priest, an experience described in *Ghosters,* the first book in Frank's saga, and an experience that still haunts him. The beginning of *Italian Girls* finds Frank feeling liberated but lonely, as well as guilty about the break-up of his marriage. He tries to find solace in love affairs with his international students at the colleges in London and Dublin where he teaches English. Ironically, though, these affairs make him realise that what he really wants is a wife and children after all. He has always had a thing for Italian girls, ever since a boyhood crush on Gina Lollobrigida, so when he falls in love with Cinzia, an Italian student, he thinks he has found the love of his life and the wife of his dreams. But has he? Or will his quest lead him to a different continent entirely ..?

'I have just finished reading Eugene Vesey's trilogy of novels, Ghosters, Opposite Worlds and Italian Girls, and have been thoroughly moved by their content. The three books are exceptionally well written, as you would expect from a scholar of English, and I would advise any reader with an interest in this problem of clerical abuse and the detritus it leaves behind to get the three.'

Paul Malpas

VENICE AND OTHER POEMS

VENICE AND OTHER POEMS is Eugene's first book of poetry. It includes poems written when he was a teenager to poems written recently. In other words, it covers a span of nearly fifty years, from his schooldays in the sixties to 2014. However, the poems are in alphabetical not chronological order. Each poem expresses a state of mind or emotion at the time, an observation of a scene or a reflection upon some experience. So in a sense the poems are autobiographical, though not necessarily an exact mirror of the author's life – there may be some 'poetic licence' here and there. Perhaps it would be better to describe each poem as a prism. As well as reflecting his own life-experience though, the author hopes that in at least some of these poems readers may catch a glimpse of their own lives, past, present or even future.

'This is a very appealing collection of poems. They are well constructed with lots of descriptive, emotive language. The writer explores deep subjects such as Love, Identity and Loss. I would recommend this collection as it has a lovely selection of poems that touch you with many emotions.'
Miss A. M. Kearney, Amazon

All Eugene's books are available from Amazon.

You can contact Eugene at:

veseyeugene@hotmail.com

www.ingramcontent.com/pod-product-compliance
Ingram Content Group UK Ltd.
Pitfield, Milton Keynes, MK11 3LW, UK
UKHW041846200726
13854UKWH00005BA/2249